Plants in Danger

PLANTS IN DANGER

by Edward R. Ricciuti

Illustrations by Ann Zwinger

Harper & Row, Publishers
New York, Hagerstown, San Francisco, London

The artist would like to thank Ruth Sumners and
Mike Ruggiero of the New York Botanical Garden, and
Dr. and Mrs. Edwin Way Teale.

PLANTS IN DANGER
Copyright © 1979 by Edward Raphael Ricciuti
Illustrations © 1979 by Ann Zwinger

Library of Congress Cataloging in Publication Data
Ricciuti, Edward R
    Plants in danger.

    SUMMARY: Discusses plant species from all parts
of the world that are in danger of extinction.
    1. Rare plants—Juvenile literature.   2. Plant
conservation—Juvenile literature.   [1. Rare plants.
2. Plant conservation]   I. Zwinger, Ann.   II. Title.
QK86.A1R5 1979   333.9′5   77-25669
ISBN 0-06-024978-1
ISBN 0-06-024979-X lib. bdg.

For the Lemons

Contents

Vanishing Plants

Two centuries ago, a tiny seed lay on the hot sand of the Arizona desert, not far from the fortified Spanish garrison town of Tucson. The seed had popped out of the red pulp of a small fruit which had ripened, fallen to the ground, and split open. Sand tossed by the desert wind covered the seed. It had escaped the notice of the hungry kangaroo rats and of the white-winged doves that landed with whirring wings. During the day the seed, now covered, was shaded by a scraggly paloverde tree which grew nearby.

The seed in the shade of the paloverde sprouted, and a tiny plant arose from it. The plant grew slowly, so slowly that even after a few years it was no taller than your finger. By the time ten years had passed, the plant had ballooned into a small greenish ball, studded with spines and scored from top to bottom with folds, like those on an accordion bellows.

More years passed. After thirty years or so, the plant that had sprouted from the little seed had reached a yard in height. It looked like a sausage standing on end. It was a cactus—but what a cactus! Already it had lived long, but its life was just beginning.

In about another half century, the cactus would stand twenty feet high, and an arm would branch from it. Mean-

1

SAGUARO CACTUS

while, the garrison of soldiers in Tucson would change, from Spanish to Mexican to American. All the while the cactus would keep growing. While Tucson developed from an adobe frontier town to a modern city, the cactus would sprout more arms, and increase in height and bulk. Finally, two centuries from the time it had sprouted, the cactus would tower fifty feet above the desert, and it would weigh ten tons.

This cactus is a saguaro, a marvelous plant found only in the Sonora Desert of northwestern Mexico, southwestern Arizona, and the fringes of southeastern California. In all the world, only there will it grow. Despite its size, the saguaro is really a very delicate plant that survives only under a special set of conditions. And it is one of the thousands of plants all over the world that are vulnerable to extinction.

Some of these plants are so rare their species are doomed, unable to reproduce. There simply are too few to produce enough offspring to continue their kind. Others still exist in relatively large numbers, but the conditions that could make them vanish are developing rapidly, so their survival is uncertain unless measures are taken to protect them.

In recent years people have become increasingly aware that many kinds of wild animals are threatened with extinction. For one reason or another, about 1,000 species of animals are in danger. The threat to the world's plant life is even greater. More than 20,000 species of plants—about a tenth of all species known to science—could disappear forever unless something is done to save them.

In the United States alone, more than 300 species of plants may already have disappeared. The Department of the Interior officially classifies almost 2,000 species as either in immediate danger of extinction or likely to become endangered before too many more years pass. Actually, the number of plants which are becoming scarce in the United States surpasses even the total on the official endangered species list.

Most of the endangered plants of the United States never were very widespread. Most live in very special types of habitat. The small Virginia round-leafed birch tree, for instance, grows only in a small area near the town of Sugar Grove, Virginia. A species of the tarweed shrub lives only on the cindery slopes of a volcano in Hawaii. In fact, most of the plants native to Hawaii are found only on those islands. Forty percent of them are in danger—more than half of the species on the Interior Department endangered list. California, Florida, and Texas also have many native plants which are on the list. At the same time, there are plants whose species have been pushed to the brink of extinction in almost every one of the fifty states.

Even plants that are in no danger of dying out as a species are becoming critically scarce in many places where they once were abundant. The jack-in-the-pulpit, for example, grows in the wet woodlands of the eastern half of the United States, and in southeastern Canada. Because the plant is so widespread there is little danger it will disappear entirely. However, the jack-in-the-pulpit has become so rare in many parts of its range that people living in these places consider it a rare plant.

Outside the United States, plant life faces similar problems. There are few places on the face of the earth where some plants are not in danger. The destruction of plant life is going on even in places like the windswept plateaus of the South American Andes, or the once-mysterious rain forests of central Africa. Scientists believe that the rate of extinction

JACK-IN-THE-PULPIT

of plant life is so rapid that many species are being lost before they are discovered, so no one really knows how many plants are disappearing.

Of course, throughout geologic history, since life appeared on earth, species of plants and animals have arisen, flourished, and then vanished. Extinction is as natural for species as survival. When a species vanishes because the climate becomes too cold for it, or because another species crowds it out, its extinction is part of the natural scheme of things. Year by year, century by century, changes occur in the earth's environment that make it more difficult for some species to survive, easier for others. Weather patterns shift. Mountain ranges arise, then erode. Sea levels advance and retreat. Desert covers landscapes where forests once grew. Trees cover land once under water. Glaciers crunch over hills and plains, then shrink to nothing. Change continually occurs in nature, although usually—but not always—major natural changes take place over very long periods of time.

Species change, as well as their environments. From time to time new traits appear by chance in living things. These new characteristics are passed along from parents to offspring. Usually such variations are not very noticeable, at least in the beginning. But sometimes they become stronger, as they continue over many generations. Eventually they may become so strong the species itself changes into a brand-new type.

So long as changes in a species help it adapt to its environment, the species is ahead in the race to survive. Because nature always changes, a species is almost always under pressure to keep up with the varying conditions around it. If it doesn't chances are it will become extinct.

Most major natural changes occur so slowly that the

extinction of species has been a gradual process. As old species fade away and new ones arise, a balance of sorts has been maintained. But today, humanity has upset that balance. Human populations have vastly increased, and spread to almost every corner of the earth. Humans need more food, shelter, and energy, in skyrocketing amounts. And at the same time, human ability to control nature has also increased. All this has meant that people are changing the environment much more quickly, and in many more ways, than is natural. Many species which had been able to keep up with natural change have not been able to adapt to the ways people have altered the environment. As a result, these species either have disappeared altogether or are vanishing fast.

Some kinds of wild animals, such as the great whales, have been overhunted. So many blue whales, the largest animals that ever lived, have been taken from the wild that not enough may be left to reproduce the species. Certain types of plants also have been removed from the wild in such great numbers that their future is in doubt. Among them are some species of orchids and cacti which are prized by plant fanciers. As far as wild animals are concerned, however, the greatest threat to survival is the destruction of habitat. Most animals are adapted to only one particular kind of habitat, or at most a few types. They can survive only in their special habitats, nowhere else. If, for example, the great rain forests of Borneo and Sumatra continue to be cut for timber, the orangutan that lives in them will vanish from the wild. Because the forest is threatened, so is the orangutan. This is a very important point, and not just about the orangutan. Plants are the key ingredients of most habitats. Often when we speak of the destruction of an animal's habitat, we mean the failure to conserve plants—those of rain forests, for example, or prairies, deserts, or wetlands. In the end, the way we conserve the plant kingdom will determine the fate of wild animals, and also quite likely of humanity.

Plants, Animals, and People

THE FIRST PLANTS were single cells that floated in the waters of the sea. Their appearance between two billion and three billion years ago marked a major change in the course of life. Until that time, the only living things had been cell-like organisms that existed on the nutrients which were naturally present in the soupy waters. But the plant cells were different. They contained a green compound called chlorophyll, which gave them an awesome new power: It enabled them to trap and harness the energy of sunlight, directly, to make their own food. These first plants did not have to depend on whatever nutrients they could find in the sea to sustain them.

With a few exceptions such as bacteria, fungi, and yeasts, plants have the unique ability to manufacture food—sugars—from the water and carbon dioxide in the environment around them. That is, they can do it as long as light is available. The process is called "photosynthesis," which means "building with light." By forming food for itself, a green plant actually converts light energy to chemical energy it can use to power its life processes.

These first green plants in turn opened up a vast new food supply, never before available to living things. Plants became storehouses of energy for themselves, and for anything that could feed upon them. Somehow, in the ancient sea, there appeared cells which could eat the plants, and all life became divided into two kingdoms. On one hand are the primary producers of food, the plants. On the other are the consumers, the animals. All animals, even meat eaters, get their energy from plants—by eating either the plants or the animals that eat plants. When a lion or tiger eats the flesh of its prey, it really is tapping the energy of the sun, originally converted into a usable form by plants.

And all the while plants are making food, they are keeping the atmosphere breathable for animal life. During photosynthesis, plants take carbon dioxide from the air and release oxygen. It was in this manner, long, long ago, that plants created the life-giving mix of gases in our air.

Today, most of the oxygen in the atmosphere is produced by the countless billions of tiny plants that swarm in the sunlit coastal waters of the sea. Although these plants are microscopic, or nearly so, they are so numerous their numbers make up for lack of size.

Two kinds of microplants are most abundant. In cold water, plants called diatoms predominate. Minuscule blobs of one cell each, diatoms use a mineral called silica, taken from sea water, to encase themselves in wondrously tiny shells. Surrounded by its lacy armor of silica, a diatom resembles a tiny jewel when seen under a microscope. In warmer water, one-celled plants called dinoflagellates are

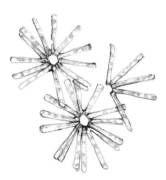

DIATOMS

common. Some of them are responsible for the so-called phosphorescence in the sea, the tiny specks of light seen in the water at night. Their light is caused by a complicated chemical reaction, just like the one that illuminates fireflies' lanterns. Others, when present in unusually large concentrations, can cause the deadly "red tide" which poisons water and kills fish.

Dinoflagellates are particularly interesting because they have the animal-like ability to swim. Some of them, like animals, even prey on other organisms. But most live by photosynthesis alone, like ordinary plants, and along with the diatoms are important producers of oxygen.

The rain forests of the tropics are the other great producer of oxygen. Not only do they do that, but they also use up so much carbon dioxide that if all the jungles were cleared, the content of that gas in the atmosphere would increase perhaps as much as ten percent. This would cause major changes in the earth's environment because carbon dioxide in the atmosphere shapes weather and even climates. A property of carbon dioxide is that it absorbs heat but has no reaction with light. So sunlight can pass through the carbon dioxide in the air. Once the sunlight strikes the earth, it is changed to heat and radiated back into the atmosphere. There the carbon dioxide absorbs the heat, warming the atmosphere. The more carbon dioxide builds up in the atmosphere, the warmer it will become.

Since the initial development of modern industrial technology about two centuries ago, carbon dioxide from the combustion of fuels has been a major part of air pollution. Some scientists worry that the increase in levels of carbon dioxide from pollutants is disrupting the patterns of climate. If forest destruction adds to the build-up, the situation could become even worse. If the average temperature of the earth's atmosphere were only a few degrees higher, the polar icecaps could melt. Sea level would rise as much as 500 feet. New York City, Los Angeles, New Orleans, Washington, D.C., and most of the other large cities on the world's coastlines would be under water.

Forests also have an influence upon the earth's water cycle. Through a process called transpiration, all green plants return their excess water to the atmosphere as vapor. Because forests contain such a vast amount of plant material, they are an important source of water vapor for the atmosphere.

Forests, by their root systems, also help keep water locked in the soil after it rains, so it will be there to supply moisture during dry periods. Scientists who cleared 37 acres of forest in New Hampshire to find out how it would affect the drainage of the area found that the runoff of water from the tract increased by almost half.

Researchers also have discovered that forests not only help store water, but actually can produce a type of "rain." This happens in forests on seacoasts swept by thick fogs, and on mountains draped by clouds and mist. Drops of moisture in the fog and clouds often are too light to fall to the earth. However, the droplets will stick to surfaces such as branches, twigs, and leaves. Once stuck, the droplets combine, grow in size, and become heavy enough to slide off and fall to the ground. "Rain" that otherwise never would fall waters the earth because of forests.

During the course of a year, a large amount of water can be provided this way. The forests of the Green Mountains of Vermont contribute five inches of "rain" yearly to the soil. Forests in the Alps of southern Germany produce 170 percent more water from the fog that often cloaks them than comes from yearly rainfall.

Thoughtless destruction of a forest can have dire effects upon an area's water supply. This is what happened on a high plateau in the mountains of southeastern Mexico. The plateau was walled by high mountains covered with forests. During the dry season, half a year long, the forests took water from the fog that rolled over the region from the Gulf of Mexico. The "rain" made by the forests watered the plateau below during the long months when no real rain fell from the sky. But then farmers, in search of more land for growing crops, cut the forests on the mountain slopes. As a result, although there is plenty of moisture in the fog that swirls overhead, none now falls to earth in the dry season. The region has become a desert, grim proof of how important plants are to the land environment.

Plants were the first living things to emerge from the sea, where life began, to "colonize" the land. The first plants ashore probably were algae, washed up on the beach. Most of them probably dried out and died, but after a while— millions and millions of years, perhaps—some managed to retain enough moisture to stay alive at the water's edge. This occurred about 600 million years ago.

Not for about 200 million years after that did the first primitive amphibians, or rather their fishlike ancestors, creep from the water. For ages, almost too long for us to imagine, plants grew and died, and enriched the soil with their remains. Eventually, gigantic swampy forests rooted themselves in the soil and covered much of the land. During the Carboniferous period, which ended about 270 million years ago, the remains of these forests partly decayed, were covered by earth and rock, and eventually formed immense coal beds. Most of the coal used today is composed of their remains. Sometimes you can see, on a piece of coal, the imprint of the leaves or stems of these plants which lived and died long before even the remote ancestors of humans appeared on earth.

A few of the plants of those ancient days still survive. Some, such as the club mosses that grow on the woodland floor, are only a fraction of the size they were in the time when great fin-backed reptiles sloshed through the swamps. Others, such as the odd ginkgo tree, are quite rare, at least in the wild. One group of trees that grew in Carboniferous times is still common. For it was then that the conifers—which now include pines, spruces, and firs—first appeared. In the ages that followed the Carboniferous, the conifers spread like a green blanket over much of the earth. Even so, the landscape would have seemed very strange to our eyes. It lacked a group of plants that has immense importance in our lives, one that gives pleasure as well as making it possible for us to survive.

Is it hard to imagine that once there was not a single flower in all the world? Not one flower to liven up the dark, green forests with its color. Nor to perfume the air. There were no fruits, either. And nowhere, on the entire surface of

leaf

GINKGO

branch with leaves and fruit

the earth, did one single blade of grass grow. That is a picture of the world until about 125 million years ago, as the Age of Reptiles was climaxing. Suddenly, somewhere in a field or forest long lost in time, a plant flowered. And the world has not been the same since.

Flowering plants, often called true seed plants because their seeds are much more sophisticated than those of conifers, quickly dominated all other vegetation. By the time the last dinosaurs had vanished, grasslands had appeared and were spreading among forests that were looking more and more like the jungles of today. Eventually, older forms of plants disappeared or retreated into out-of-the-way corners, crowded out by the ever-advancing armies of the grasses, the new trees and bushes, the vines and wildflowers.

Flowering plants surged ahead because their advanced way of reproduction permitted them to spread very rapidly. Very primitive plants, such as mosses, reproduce in hit-or-miss fashion. They release dustlike spores, at the mercy of the wind and weather. Only if a spore happens to land in the right place, under the right conditions, does it produce a tiny plant, which must immediately obtain nutrients or die. Flowering plants, and conifers as well, give their offspring a head start. They have seeds. A seed is a marvel. It really is an infant plant, contained with a food supply within hard walls. It is prepackaged for survival, protected until it sprouts, and supplied with the food it needs to start life on its own.

Conifer seeds, shelved until they are released between the scales of woody cones, are "naked"—that is, they have no protection but their own walls. The seeds of flowering plants grow deep within the flower, inside a tiny container called a

13

BLUE SPRUCE

cone

seeds

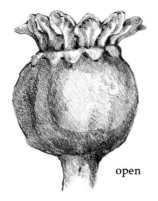

open

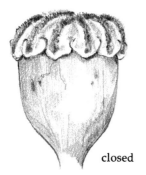

closed

POPPY
capsule

carpel, which is the female part of the flower. The carpel might shelter only one seed, but usually contains many within its covering. As the seeds grow, the carpel changes. It becomes a fruit, although not always a "fruit" as we generally use the word, as in the case of a peach or strawberry. Fruits may be leathery, brittle, tough, or hard, as well as juicy and fleshy. The pod of a bean or pea is a fruit. So is a walnut, and the capsule of a poppy. The fruit of grasses, which include cereals such as corn, is merely the thin, delicate covering of the grain.

Fruits not only protect seeds while they are forming, but also play an important role in distributing them. Many fruits are eaten by animals. As the animals feed they may drop seeds to the ground, or spit them out. Some seeds are adapted to pass undamaged through animal digestive tracts, and are left in the droppings. Fruits such as bean pods dry out and burst when ripe, tossing their seeds all about them. Other fruits, small ones, have burrs or hooks that snag on

PENNYCRESS
seed pods

LOCUST
seed pods

COCKLEBUR
seed with burrs

the coats of passing animals. Some have "wings" or "parachutes," and are carried by the wind.

The fruits of many plants provide valuable sources of food for animals. Even flesh-eating animals such as jaguars sometimes feed upon jungle fruits. Seeds are marvelous storehouses of energy. Ounce for ounce, pound for pound, no other plants come close to the flowering plants in terms of the food energy they supply to animals. Only flowering plants, in fact, can supply the stupendous amounts of energy needed to fuel the high-powered bodily processes of most warm-blooded creatures. Birds and mammals, unlike other animals, maintain their body temperatures internally. But to do it, they must produce lots of body heat. This means, for example, that a squirrel burns up immeasurably more food energy than a snake, frog, or other cold-blooded creature.

It was not only the extinction of the dinosaurs and other great reptiles that gave warm-blooded creatures like birds and mammals their chance to inherit the earth. What also

Seeds with "wings"

MAPLE
seeds

Seeds with "parachutes"

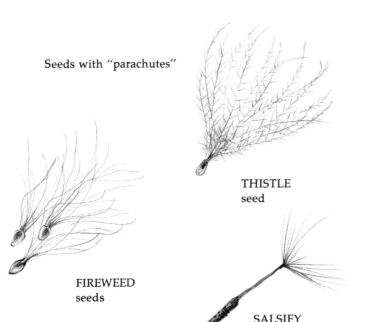

THISTLE
seed

FIREWEED
seeds

SALSIFY
seed

AILANTHUS
seeds

made it possible was the appearance, more than 100 million years ago, of flowers. As had happened before in history, plants had opened up a whole new food supply for animals.

The crops that farmers plant today all are descended from wild plants. Of them all, the most important to people are the grasses. Often we think of grasses merely as plants growing on lawns, or perhaps in parks and meadows, too. Actually there are 10,000 different species of grasses, and they grow all over the world in places where there is not too much shade and where the weather is not extremely cold. Grasses come in many forms and sizes. Bamboo, which towers over the jungle floor in high tropical and subtropical mountains, is a grass. So is sugar cane. Corn, rice, barley, wheat, and all the other cereals are grasses. The grains of wheat, corn, and other cereals which are the basic foods of most people ripen in the tiny flowers of these grasses. They are particularly important because the grains are crammed full of starch, a key part of the human diet, especially in the form of flour.

During the course of human history, people have used more than 3,000 species of plants for food. Today most of the world's food supply comes from about 15 different types of plants, especially wheat, rice, corn, and sorghum. Most of the varieties of food plants today have been specially bred to produce the greatest yields of food, at the expense of their hardiness. They are as removed from their sturdy wild ancestors as fat beef cattle are from the wild, agile aurochs, the huge, now-extinct wild ox from which domestic cattle originated. As the world's grasslands are opened up to agriculture, increasing numbers of wild grasses are disappearing, to make room for their domestic relatives.

It might seem beneficial to create new farmlands, especially in the world's tropics, where most of the world's poorer and more densely populated nations are located. According to the United Nations Food and Agricultural Organization, within just a few years at least 26 tropical nations with a total population of 365 million will not have enough food to avoid gradual starvation. But if wild grasses are eliminated, a danger of even greater starvation hangs over the world. Less hardy than the wild plants, many domestic varieties are more likely to catch diseases. Although most crop diseases can be treated and controlled, the fearful chance always exists that a new, untreatable disease can strike, swiftly and without warning. If it swept through just one of the world's major grain crops, starvation on a scale never before seen could result. One way of coping with such a problem would be to interbreed the domestic plant with a stronger wild relative that is able to resist disease. That possibility, conservationists say, is more than enough reason to safeguard wild grasses from extinction. In our haste to feed hungry people today, we must not endanger plant resources that could prove livesavers in the future. This is true of many other domesticated plants besides grains. If the forests of Africa are leveled, all of the wild kinds of coffee will vanish. Wild bananas will disappear with the jungles of southeast Asia. Wild cashew nuts, cacao, and rubber depend on the survival of tropical American forests.

The destruction of plant life threatens not only food resources, but important medicines, too. Most people realize how much humans depend upon plants for food, but do not realize that we also use plants for medicine. Many kinds of plants furnish chemicals which are the basis for medicines which have saved countless human lives. Some of these medicines have been known to tribal medicine men for centuries, but only recently have they been discovered by modern physicians.

Bush doctors of certain West African tribes, for example, have used a plant called rauwolfia to calm people upset mentally. Elsewhere in the tropics, the same plant has many other medicinal uses, including treatment of snakebite. After years of testing rauwolfia, physicians have discovered that the plant really does produce compounds useful in modern medicine. These have been used to help calm people with mental disorders, and to lower high blood pressure.

Many other plants have helped heal diseases, either by producing chemicals which can be used directly or by serving as models for medicines reproduced in the laboratory. A brief sample will give an idea of how important plants are in modern medicine. Curare, a poison made from a vine that South American Indians use to tip their hunting darts, has proved to be a very helpful drug in surgery. It relaxes the muscles and serves as an anesthetic. Digitalis, used to regulate an irregular heartbeat, is based on a chemical found in the foxglove flower. Synthetic versions of curare and digitalis have been developed. Penicillin—and, indeed, most modern antibiotic drugs—are produced by microscopic molds, very simple plants usually found in the soil. Hormones from wild yams have been used to treat arthritis, rheumatism, serious burns, and skin infections. The bark of the cinchona tree, a South American plant, is the source of quinine, which for centuries—until very recently—was the only treatment for malaria.

Scientists believe that among the countless unidentified species of plants, there are many which might produce medically useful chemicals. Some scientists believe that as many as 50,000 useful chemicals await discovery in plants.

FOXGLOVE
flower

Who knows which of the serious diseases that still afflict humanity could be treated by compounds found in plants which may be destroyed even before they are known to science? By eliminating plants we are destroying not only something that can benefit us, but the very environment on which we depend for life. No species vanishes without in some way—good or bad—affecting the environment on which all life is based. Because, in the end, all species are linked in the web of life, the unnatural extinction of any one breaks down the system. The disappearance of a single plant may not have a drastic effect upon the natural system, but when many plants disappear over a short period of time, the results can be very serious. This is particularly true of plants, because their existence is so basic to the survival of animal life. To a very great degree, plants make the environment.

The War Against the Plants

THE WAR WAGED by humanity against the plant kingdom is going on all over the world. In South America, farmers burn off piece after piece of jungle. In Minnesota, trees and flowers have been shriveled by air pollution. On the Arizona desert, plant collectors dig up rare cacti. In New Jersey, rare bog plants disappear amidst housing and industrial developments. Even in the sea, plants are being destroyed as the coastal waters supporting microplants such as diatoms and dinoflagellates are being polluted.

The prairies of the American west, which once covered a third of the United States, have all but vanished. Many prairie plants are so rare they must be maintained in preserves. Most of the vast grasslands of east Africa have been carved up into small farms and ranches. In many parts of Kenya and Tanzania, where tall grasses once waved, cattlemen have allowed their livestock to feed until all vegetation has disappeared, and the plains and rolling hills are barren. The low-growing plants of the bleak plateaus of South America's Andes have suffered the same fate. And in much of the Himalayan mountain range, villagers have taken every twig for firewood, while their goats and sheep devour the last greenery.

Wetlands, too, are disappearing, piece by piece in some

places, all at once in others. Connecticut lost half its coastal wetlands in small parcels over the last half century. New York's coastal wetlands decreased almost thirty percent between 1954 and 1964. The Everglades, which once covered almost all of south Florida, have been so disrupted by drainage systems that only a tenth of this watery wilderness remains.

The destruction of the plant kingdom has been under way for about 10,000 years, since the beginnings of agriculture, but it began very slowly. Long after civilizations arose in the Middle East and around the Mediterranean, tall pines and oaks still grew in southern Italy, Sicily, and Greece. The rugged mountains of northwestern Iran and eastern Turkey were covered with deep forests. In Israel, Lebanon, and Syria, hillsides were covered with green grass and dotted with trees. But by 2,000 years ago, these regions were already being devastated. Livestock had eaten the seedling trees, so when the old trees died, nothing replaced them. The last large trees were cut for timber. The grass was eaten away by hungry sheep, cattle, and goats.

As the trees and the grass disappeared, the soil lost its protection against erosion by wind and water. It was stripped away, in many places to the bare rock. Today the hills and mountains of the Middle East are brown, bare, and dusty. Where the tall trees grew in southern Europe, only scrub can now be seen.

A truly vast forest, dark and primitive, once covered almost all of central and western Europe. But most of it has vanished, too. Its destruction began after the fall of Rome. At first this destruction was piecemeal, as towns, castles, and farms appeared among the endless trees. By the end of the Middle Ages, however, the forest was only a memory, except high in the mountains and in a few special preserves.

One such preserve is in eastern Poland. Known as the Bialowieza National Park, it is the last scrap of the ancient forest left in central Europe. The Bialowieza forest is carefully tended by government foresters, and a few foreign trees have been introduced there, but for the most part it looks much as it did 2,000 years ago. Amidst the dark stands of pine and spruce are scattered thick, spreading oaks, their trunks often eight feet in diameter, and white-barked birches. Walking through the sun-dappled glades and shadowed depths of this forest, surrounded by gnarled and ancient tree trunks, the observer can easily understand why fairy tales and other old stories from the Middle Ages often told of the forest as a spooky place, a realm of mystery.

When Columbus discovered America, what is now the United States from the Atlantic to the Mississippi was covered by a vast, virgin forest of towering trees, broken only by natural glades, wetlands, a few patches of prairie, and the clearings of woodland Indians. It has been estimated that there were 800 million acres of virgin forest in the United States before the coming of the Europeans almost five centuries ago. Today, less than 10 percent remains, and the eastern forests consist largely of runty second- and third-growth trees—the smaller types which grow after a field begins to turn to woodland.

Only a century ago, a great belt of green encircled the middle of the earth. It was the vast tropical jungle—actually a band of many different types of forests, especially the wet kind known as rain forest. Today the belt is tattered and broken. Perhaps nowhere else on earth can the increased speed with which the plant world is being destroyed be so easily seen. This is because the destruction is taking place on a massive scale, as bulldozers and other modern machines become available in tropical lands. It is a battle of titans, huge growling machines against ancient, towering trees.

Forests in places once considered impenetrable, such as the Amazon, are being penetrated by highways. On the highways come settlers, farmers, and industries. In Central America, coffee and banana plantations have replaced forests over vast regions. The jungle that remains grows only in the interiors of deep canyons and on very steep peaks. On Puerto Rico and the other islands of the West Indies—once largely jungle covered—mountaintops hold the only really deep forests, and these are ringed with farms and towns. In the Aberdare Mountains of Kenya, now a national park, the forest is surrounded on all sides by farms. The farms have come so close to the park boundary that a ditch has had to be dug around it to keep out livestock. Thailand, once a jungle country, has little forest left. In many parts of the nation there are no more large trees. Yet in a few places—mostly preserves, back country, or national parks—a traveler can see what it must have been like.

Outside the preserves, the destruction of the tropical rain forests goes on as if they were endless. Indonesia, for example, has allowed uncontrolled logging on 67 million acres, a region the size of Colorado. In Colombia, the rate of rain-forest destruction amounts to four acres every minute, each day, all year round. The destruction of the jungle on a worldwide scale is even worse, and four times that rate.

The Last Forest Giants
and Other Threatened Trees

A HUNDRED MILLION years ago, the world was populated by giants. Dinosaurs and other great reptiles were at the peak of their development. But animals were not the only giants of that lost age. Throughout the northern hemisphere, a group of giant trees grew. Their trunks were massive columns, rising straight to the sky. Their branches were themselves as large as big trees. They were plants to match the giant beasts of the times.

The giant trees were sequoias, or redwoods. For millions of years they flourished in North America, Europe, and Asia. The dinosaurs vanished, but the sequoias still stood, although newer types replaced older varieties. Mammals prospered and spread over the world. And still the sequoias waved their lofty crowns in the wind. Humans appeared, and more than likely looked up in awe at the mighty trees. Then came a series of ice sheets, crunching down from the north and the high mountains. It was a cold time, and at last the range of the sequoias began to shrink. The big trees lost ground before the cold until they survived only in isolated pockets instead of the range their kind had owned before. Today, only two kinds of sequoia survive, the coast redwood and giant sequoia, both of which grow in California. The coast redwood, common in North America and western

Europe during past ages, now grows only on the rain-soaked, misty Pacific coast between San Francisco and the Oregon border. The giant sequoia rises from the western slopes of the Sierra Nevada, at altitudes between 4,000 and 8,000 feet where, in winter, snow descends like a vast white blanket. The giant sequoia never was as widespread as its relatives, but even so in prehistoric times could be found through much of western North America.

Thousands of years old, and so huge they stagger the imagination, the giant sequoias and redwoods are kings of the plant world. The largest sequoias alive today began growing before the Greeks and Trojans fought under the walls of Troy, even before Moses led his people out of Egypt. The oldest redwoods date at least to the time of Christ.

The redwood is the slimmer of the two species, but generally taller. One discovered in 1966 reaches a height of 385 feet. Sequoias are not as high—the tallest known is 272 feet—although in the past they may have grown much more lofty. Based on the remains of its trunk, an old fallen sequoia known as the "father of the forest" may have stood 400 feet above the ground. However, it is the bulk of the giant sequoia, rather than its height, that makes it the largest of all living things. The trunk of a giant sequoia can be more than 100 feet around at its base—more than 30 feet in diameter. Hollowed out, an old trunk can be literally as big as a house, and indeed, people have lived within sequoia trunks.

Once it begins to grow to even moderate size, a giant sequoia or redwood is almost indestructible. The bark of these tremendous plants, almost a foot thick on old trees, is too tough for most fires to penetrate. The wood resists insects and diseases. People really are the only enemy of the forest giants.

SEQUOIA
twig

25

Ever since the American frontier was pushed to the Pacific, the redwoods and sequoias have steadily diminished, so that today conservationists fear for the survival of these reminders of prehistoric times. Both grow in groves from a few to hundreds of trees. Of the two, however, the redwoods are more common and occupy a much wider area, so until rather recently most of the attention has been given to saving the giant sequoia.

The threat to the giant sequoia began oddly enough and by chance, on a spring day in 1852. A hunter from a mining camp in the foothills of the Sierras had been tracking a grizzly bear into the high country. On the trail of the bear, which he had wounded, the hunter—Augustus T. Dowd— wandered into a part of the forest strange to him. As he moved quietly through the woodland, he suddenly encountered a sight that undoubtedly left him awestruck. He had entered a grove of trees unlike any he had ever seen before. They were gargantuan, fantastic, too huge for words.

Dowd had discovered the giant sequoias—which of course, Indians living in the region had known about all along—but when he returned to camp nobody believed him. After some of the miners trekked back into the mountains to see the trees described by Dowd, though, the news quickly spread, not just through the California gold camps but across the country, and then to Europe.

The so-called big trees quickly became a tourist attraction. One group of five men immediately set out to fell one of the giants. It took them more than three weeks. Once it was down they stripped off pieces of bark, which were sent to New York City for display. Bark from another tree was shipped to London.

Lumbermen rapidly responded to the lure of the big trees

as other groves were discovered up and down a 250-mile strip along the west slope of the Sierras. Cutting down huge trees growing in mile-high mountains was no easy task, but the loggers persisted, for the sequoias seemed to offer a boundless supply of lumber. The trouble was, however, that once a big tree hit the ground it shattered into small pieces. This did not discourage the loggers. Sequoia wood was everlasting. Even broken into small pieces it made excellent stakes for fences and vegetables, shingles and poles.

By the turn of the century, thousands of giant sequoias had been cut. The biggest were left lying on the ground because they were too difficult to handle. At this time loggers leveled what was probably the most beautiful of all the giant sequoia groves, in an area called Converse Basin. They cut every single tree. Never again will giant sequoias grow naturally in Converse Basin. The seeds of the sequoia travel only a short distance from the parent tree, so for new sequoias to sprout, old ones must be nearby.

For such a mighty monarch of plants, the giant sequoia begins life in a very small way. The naked seeds, which are formed within small cones, are not much larger than the period at the end of this sentence. The seeds appear in the winter, and are fertilized as the cold winds blow the sequoia pollen in dusty puffs and clouds. After three years the cones open and the seeds—sometimes more than 300 to a cone—drop or are carried a short way from the parent tree by the breeze.

Few of the seeds sprout. Most are eaten by birds and rodents. Many are infertile. Out of those that are fertile, perhaps only one in a million becomes a seedling. And the seedlings are as delicate as the grown trees indestructible. They are at the mercy of the weather and of an army of

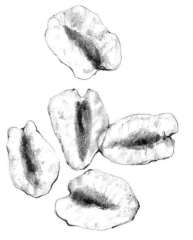

SEQUOIA
seeds

27

animals, from deer to insects, which eat them. Moreover, the seedlings need plenty of light, which is not always available in the forest. The seedlings have the best chance if shortly before the seeds are sown, a fire sweeps through the forest, clearing out the low brush and small trees that block the sunlight from the ground. But if fire comes after the seedlings sprout, they are killed.

Fires set by sheepmen to clear the forests for their livestock killed countless young sequoias at the same time the loggers were attacking the larger trees. This meant that both the existing and future generations of sequoias would be doomed unless the destruction was stopped.

Even as some people were eliminating the sequoias, though, others were trying to save them. As early as 1879, some federal officials were demanding protection for the big trees, and groups of citizens in California were organizing to stop their destruction. Slowly, a piece at a time, over many years, the sequoia groves were designated as parks and preserves. But all the while not only were people cutting trees outside the sanctuaries, but many loggers ignored the law and even cut sequoias within the boundaries of the reserves. At times the United States Cavalry had to be used to protect the trees.

During the first decades of this century, with the organization of the National Forest Service and National Park Service, protection of the sequoias became more assured. With government and private money, more sequoia groves were purchased. The process continued until quite recently, and as late as 1954 a large grove of giant sequoias was purchased from a lumber company and added to a California national park, established not far from where Augustus T. Dowd had first seen the giant trees.

Today all but a few giant sequoias are on state or federal lands, in parks such as Yosemite, Sequoia, and Kings Canyon, and in the Tahoe National Forest. It might seem as if the giant sequoias are safe, that years from now people still will be able to see the forest giants. Perhaps, but not without constant watchfulness. People concerned with the conservation of nature can never sit back and rest. The battles won, the work of years, can be undone in no time at all. The sequoias, for example, are no longer threatened by logging, but their future is by no means certain. In a sense, the remaining sequoias have been protected too well. Forest fires, necessary to clear out the trees that otherwise shade the sequoia seedlings, have been controlled so well the young sequoias do not get enough sunlight. Conservationists say better programs of controlled burning are needed, now that the natural cycle of fire and growth, which worked so well before humans upset the ecological balance, has been disrupted.

Even the interest people have in the sequoias has worked against the big trees. The sequoias, for all their size, have roots that spread over the ground, rather than anchoring themselves deep in the soil. Normally, the balanced weight of the trees keeps them upright, but the hordes of tourists visiting the groves, and the traffic that results, is packing the soil, changing the stability of the ground in which the trees are rooted. There are fears that this may cause some of the trees to fall before their time. Moreover, the flood of tourists has triggered widespread activity—the building of camps, for instance—which conservationists say could disturb the ecological balance of the surrounding area.

The web of life in a forest is so extensive that often it is difficult to preserve a stand of trees without also preserving a large portion of the forest around it. This fact has been grimly demonstrated by what has happened to the relative of the sequoia, the coast redwood.

The redwood belt, more than thirty miles wide in some places, covers about two million acres of wet, fog-swept land up to 2,000 feet in altitude. Since the early Spanish explorers—the first Europeans to see the redwoods—visited the belt two centuries ago, its boundaries have changed little. But within its boundaries, the redwood forest bears little resemblance to the vast virgin woodland that once grew there. Today, only about 150,000 acres of untouched redwood forest with the towering, ancient trees survive. And except for 50,000 acres in national and state sanctuaries, the rest is being logged so fast it may disappear within a few years. This is not to say, of course, that redwoods have vanished from the remainder of the belt. They have not. Redwoods are scattered in groves throughout the same range as before. But outside of those virgin 150,000 acres the redwoods are young, second-growth trees hundreds of years away from their full size. Moreover, they probably will be cut by timber companies long before they attain it.

Like the sequoias, the redwoods came under attack in the years following the California gold rush of 1849. Because the lumber from the redwood is so long-lasting, and does not shatter like sequoia timber, it is extremely valuable. So for more than a century, timber companies have cut as much redwood as possible with little thought for the future. As logging has become mechanized, the rate at which the redwoods have been felled has increased to more than 10,000 acres of trees a year.

Down through the years, conservationists have fought hard, but largely without success, to stop the wholesale destruction of mature redwoods. The timber companies and loggers who worry about losing jobs have fought just as hard to stop the creation of redwood sanctuaries. The companies have been largely victorious in recent years. Political pressure from the timber companies, for example, forced the government to shrink the proposed boundaries of Redwood National Park when it was established in 1968. The park took in three existing California state parks and a large tract of new land. But the new land contained only sixteen square miles of virgin redwood forest.

Much of that primeval forest lies in valleys along stream beds. Above, on the slopes, land that drains into the streams was not included in the park, despite pleas from conservationists. They had argued that the slopes and the trees below formed a single ecological unit. If the slopes were not protected and logging took place there, the conservationists warned, the "protected" redwoods would be in danger too. Once the trees were cleared from the slopes, nothing would slow the runoff of water after rains. Floods would sweep down on the trees below. It had happened before. In 1955, hundreds of giant redwoods were toppled and broken when a flood swept water, mud, and rocks from a logged slope above the stand.

Conservationists are trying to have watersheds on the slopes included in Redwood National Park, but timber companies are still leveling the forests on the slopes. Stands of protected redwoods are surrounded by scenes of unbelievable destruction. Broken and splintered stumps, boughs and fallen tree trunks litter barren, eroded hillsides, virtually to the park borders. A grim race is on between conservationists who want the watersheds protected and the lumber companies that are clearing the slopes as fast as they can, making them useless for park land. The conservationists are losing, and so are the redwoods.

The threat to the redwoods, although serious, can be stopped. It simply is a matter of mustering enough public and political support to control the wasteful way in which the trees are harvested, and to save the watersheds. Often the solution to saving a tree in danger is not nearly as obvious. This is especially true when the threat does not come from a direct human action, such as logging, but from something more complex, such as a change in the environment, or a disease.

A disease which no one has been able to control is the reason for the near extinction of one of the most useful and majestic trees of the eastern United States, the American chestnut. The story of the chestnut's downfall shows what can happen when a disease or other harmful agent is

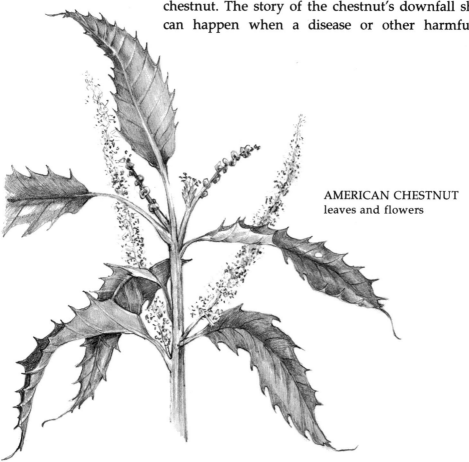

AMERICAN CHESTNUT
leaves and flowers

accidentally introduced into a country from abroad. The tale begins in 1904, and oddly enough in New York City's Bronx Park, the home of two institutions famed in conservation: the Bronx Zoo and New York Botanical Gardens.

The zoo, which today still is dotted with tall trees and patches of woodland, had a fine collection of chestnuts growing on its grounds. One day officials at the zoo noticed that the chestnuts seemed to be sick. Open, dripping sores were eating into their dark-brown bark. An expert from the botanical gardens, across the park, was called to examine the chestnuts. He found they had been attacked by a fungus. It produced sores called cankers, which spread around the trunk in a ring. The cankers destroyed the bark and finally girdled the trunk, cutting off the supply of nutrients carried just inside the bark from the roots to the upper tree. As a result, the tree above the ring of cankers withered and died.

It was an alarming situation—not only because the zoo's trees were dying, but also because the fungus that was killing them was a strange, new type. It never had been seen before. Eight years later it was discovered on another species of chestnuts, in China. Scientists in the United States decided that the fungus had probably entered this country on plants imported from Asia as ornamentals.

The Asian chestnuts, it later turned out, had been exposed to the fungus for ages, and had developed resistance to it. But, as is so often the case when a plant or animal is exposed to a brand-new disease, the American chestnut had absolutely no defense against the fungus from Asia.

At that time, the American chestnut was the most valuable tree in the forests of the eastern United States. A hundred feet high, six feet in diameter near its base, it was known for a spread of branches almost as broad as the tree was tall. Its lumber was valuable, and especially useful because it resisted decay. Its nuts provided food for wildlife, fodder for livestock and a treat for people. Vast numbers of chestnuts dominated the hardwood forests from New England, all along the Appalachian Mountains, to Alabama. They were all to perish.

The fungus disease is spread by spores, carried by the wind or on birds and other animals. The spores find their way into cracks and openings in the chestnut bark. Once they settle, the spores grow into thick blankets of fungus within the inner bark that grow toward the surface. By the time the spores appear, the tree already is dying because its sap and water supplies have been choked off by the mats of fungus.

The disease spread rapidly, at a rate of about twenty miles a year. Grand old chestnuts in New York, Connecticut, New Jersey, and Pennsylvania were among the first to go. Their leaves fell, leaving them like barren skeletons in the green forest. Within a few years, scientists recognized that all of the chestnuts were threatened.

"Unless something now unforeseen occurs to check its spread, the complete destruction of the chestnut orchards and forests of this country, or at least the Atlantic states, is only a question of time," warned an official of the United States Department of Agriculture, as early as 1908.

AMERICAN CHESTNUT

burr

chestnut

empty burr

His prediction was on target. The chestnut blight, as the disease is called, continued to spread. In 1911 Pennsylvania tried a drastic measure to stop it. Like firemen trying to halt a brush fire, scientists had a band of chestnut trees cut ahead of the blight as it advanced south through Pennsylvania. But they did not cut quickly enough, and the disease swept into the southern Appalachians.

Sprays and chemical injections were tried to combat the blight, but none of these worked. As the years passed, the mighty chestnuts continued to die. Windstorms knocked down many of the dead trees. Throughout the eastern woodlands, the rotting trunks, uprooted by storms of years past, can be seen lying like fallen giants. Some of the stumps that remain standing are fringed by suckers, young trees that have sprouted from the dead adult. But sooner or later as the young ones grow, the spores of the fungus find and destroy them.

Meanwhile, oriental chestnuts have been planted in orchards in the United States. They produce delightful nuts, but are not nearly as impressive, as trees, as the American species, nor do they produce such useful lumber. However, scientists have not given up trying to defeat the blight and restore the American species.

Here and there in the eastern forests, and in the west as well, a few chestnuts have survived, by chance, out of the millions that died. Perhaps some of these trees developed a resistance to the blight. They have furnished cuttings for scientists to graft onto Asian chestnuts, in hopes of producing a hybrid that will survive in the wild, having the resistance of the Asian species and the magnificence of the American.

Recently, another possibility for defeating the blight has been discovered in Europe. The blight appeared in Europe—

which has its own species of chestnut—several decades after it first attacked trees in the United States. Like the American chestnuts, those of Europe suffered greatly. However, after a while some of the European trees showed signs of resisting the blight. At first, scientists paid little attention, thinking it just a chance occurrence. But gradually, the blight seemed to show increasing signs it was slowing.

Scientists investigated. Eventually, French researchers discovered what had happened to curb the disease in the European chestnuts. They found that a slightly altered form of the fungus had appeared. It grows much more slowly than the usual strain of chestnut blight. The cankers are not nearly as large, and the damage to the trees much less, allowing them to heal. Moreover, the weaker new strain of fungus easily crosses with the older type, and slows its growth, too.

Strains of the weaker fungus have been shipped to scientists in the United States, who have tested them. The weak strain was placed in chestnut bark alongside the more destructive type. The difference between the two in rate of growth was clearly visible.

Although scientists have much to learn about the new strain of fungus, they already believe that it may be possible to use it to control the blight. The weak strain could be spread artificially in the woodlands, where it could combine with the more powerful type. The result would be a much less damaging type of fungus. The chestnut suckers and young trees that remain would have a much better chance of surviving its attacks.

One thing scientists have learned about the new type of fungus is that it has probably been weakened because it in turn has been infected—by a tiny viruslike agent. The organism believed responsible is known as a mycovirus, and it is found only in fungi. If indeed a mycovirus is what slows the growth of the fungus, and the agent can be isolated by scientists, perhaps it could be spread as a biological control over the blight.

Years of patient research, after all hope seemed gone, now show signs of producing results. Although it is still too early to say for sure, perhaps by the first decades of the next century great chestnut trees will again stand in the forests of the eastern United States.

The same southeastern mountains once dominated by chestnuts also are the home of what may be the rarest tree in the United States—the Ashe's, or Virginia round-leafed, birch. Only one small stand of round-leafed birches is known to exist. It was rediscovered in 1975 along a creek in southwestern Virginia, ending years of debate by botanists over whether the birch was extinct. Behind the discovery of the stand of birches lies a story, which began in 1914.

That year, a forester named William Ashe announced that he had found a new type of birch near a stream called Dickey Creek in the Blue Ridge, where Virginia narrows into a wedge between Kentucky and Tennessee. The new tree had dark bark, like the common river birch, but unlike other birches had leaves that were round, not pointed. Some time later—although exactly when is uncertain—another man, Horace B. Ayres, found another of the new birches on a nearby stream called Cressy Creek.

Ayres' find seems to have been all but forgotten, but botanists made note of the discovery by Ashe, and recognized the birch as a new species. But in the years that followed, scientists lost track of the new birch—and no one seemed able to find it again. Some botanists began to doubt it had ever existed, calling it a hoax. The official view of the United States Department of the Interior was that the birch probably was extinct.

Even so, some botanists kept searching for the birch, especially around Dickey Creek, where it first had been reported. But look as they might, they had no luck. Then, a few years ago, a young scientist on the staff of the National Arboretum in Washington, D.C., took up the search. He assembled all the information on the birch he could find, but most of it was very old, dating to the time when the birch was first reported. At that time, some leaves of the birch had been given to Harvard University and a few other institutions. The young researcher asked to see some of the leaves from Harvard. They were brought out of storage and sent to him.

Some of the leaf specimens from Harvard, it turned out, had been collected not by Ashe, but by Ayres. At least that was what a label on them stated. The label also explained that the specimen came not from Dickey Creek, but Cressy Creek. This information, forgotten for so many years, opened the door to the rediscovery of the birch when it came to the attention of a biology teacher, at a small college in southwestern Virginia, who had lived all his life in the area. The teacher, a candidate for a graduate degree in botany, began to search Cressy Creek in hopes that some of the mysterious birches still grew there. And one day he struck pay dirt. By the side of the creek, where it bordered a main highway, he found several of the birches. Scientists who have examined the site have found more than a dozen larger trees, and several seedlings. Some of the seedlings have been transplanted and taken to research institutions, where botanists will try to grow them. Researchers are also trying to grow the birches from seeds collected in the grove by the creek, which stands on private property amidst a national forest. The property owners have erected a fence around the grove to protect it, and scientists are searching the forest nearby to see if more of the birches are growing there.

For scientists, however, the mystery of the round-leafed birch is not over. It is unlike any other birch of the southern Appalachians, but closer to small birches which grow in the wet woods of the northern states. Yet as far as anyone knows, the round-leafed grows only in southwestern Virginia. Scientists would like to know why.

One possible explanation may be that during the ice ages, when the climate of the southeast was colder than today, many types of northern birch, among them the round-leafed, grew there. When the glaciers retreated, so did the birches. A few of the round-leafed species may have remained in the Blue Ridge, almost 3,000 feet up in the mountains. The climate is cooler there than in the surrounding lowlands, and more like that of the northern states. Perhaps a small colony of round-leafed birches survived for thousands of years in the Blue Ridge, while the rest of the species not only retreated, but vanished. The rediscovery of the round-leafed birch has opened up some fascinating questions.

Plants such as the round-leafed birch, which are confined to only one habitat of limited area, are very vulnerable. It makes little difference how numerous such species are within the small areas in which they are found. A natural disaster such as a bad storm, or a change in the environment caused by human activity—construction of highways, for instance—could wipe out such a species in a single stroke.

Many trees are in such a situation. There is a species of fir said to exist only as a single tree on Sicily. In Japan, a species of spruce, *Picea koyamai*, does not exist outside of a single grove. Almost all of the nearly 4,000 species of palms are limited to very restricted ranges. Of the 112 species of palms on Madagascar, for example, all but two live only there— that is, in technical terms, they are "endemic" to Madagascar. A species of small palms known by the scientific name *Salacca flabellata* is endemic only to one of the states of Malayasia. Two other Malayasian palms, *Maxburretia rupicola* and *Liberbaileya lankawiensis*, live only in a particular range of limestone hills. In fact, each palm is found only upon its own particular hill. The hills were part of a range of limestone that in ages past was more widespread. Perhaps the palms had a much wider range then, too.

Some species of palms have been almost eliminated because people have cut them down for the very tasty leaves, or "cabbage," in the heart of the crown. This has happened to palms endemic to Guadalupe, an island in the Pacific off Mexico; the Seychelle Islands of the Indian Ocean; and the tiny Bonin Islands of Japan, where during World War II hungry soldiers ate almost every palm they could find.

Several species of trees that are endemic to limited localities have been cultivated and spread to other areas, thereby taking them out of danger. The dawn redwood, a relative of the sequoias, is one of these. The dawn redwood was discovered in 1941 in China. Only a few wild trees remain, but others are cultivated in many parts of the world. So is the ancient ginkgo tree, which is also found wild only in a very few parts of central China. The 120-foot-high ginkgo is a true living fossil. It is the last survivor of a group of trees that ranged through much of the world as far back as 270 million years ago. For centuries it was cultivated on the grounds of Chinese temples, after it had almost disappeared in the wild. The cultivated trees were spread to many parts of the world as ornamentals, particularly to line streets and sidewalks. The ginkgo, although almost lost in the wild, is in no danger of vanishing as a species.

Many other trees that have been transplanted to foreign homes are more numerous there than in the places where they are found naturally. There is no better example than the flamboyant, a tree whose flaming orange-red blooms are a favorite flower of Puerto Rico. The flamboyant adds a blaze of color to the landscape of Puerto Rico, and in fact to almost every other tropical country in the world. As a wild tree, however, it grows only in one forest preserve on Madagascar, where it was discovered in 1824.

The cedar of Lebanon, famed in the ancient world for its timber, also depends on preserves for its existence in its native land. Large cedars grow in two protected groves, which over the years have drawn countless pilgrims and tourists, because the 100-foot-high trees are a living link with history.

When the pyramids were being built in Egypt, when the Israelites settled in the Promised Land, and when the Phoenicians spread the use of the modern alphabet, the rocky mountains of Lebanon were covered with thick stands of tall cedars. The logs of the cedars were a precious item of trade

leaf

GINKGO

fruit

flowering branch
with beginning leaves

for the people of the seacoast in the shadow of the mountains, people who were known first as Canaanites and then as Phoenicians. Egypt, which lacked timber, was importing cedar logs as long ago as 3,000 B.C. The logs were highly valued because they contained a resin that resisted rot. A cedar trunk uncovered by a landslide on a Lebanese mountainside in 1961, for example, was found to be almost 3,000 years old, and in perfect condition.

Cedar was the timber used for the war fleets of the ancient Egyptians and Assyrians, and the trading vessels of the far-ranging Phoenicians. Boats built of cedar carried Persian soldiers over the sea to attack Greece, and much later sped the Arab corsairs over the waves as they harried the shores of the Mediterranean.

Logs felled in the Lebanese mountains were carried by ship to Egypt and made into beams for pyramids and temples. Cedar wood was used by the Egyptians for the cases in which mummies of their kings, queens, and princes were put to rest. Temples containing cedar timbers could be found throughout the ancient world, from Carthage to Assyria. David and his son Solomon, kings of Israel, built palaces of the fine-scented wood that came from the mountains that rose north of their borders.

Of all the ancient monuments and buildings that contained cedar the most famous was the temple of Solomon at Jerusalem. Although a few historians suggest that perhaps juniper wood was used instead, tradition, the Bible, and most scholars agree that the temple was built with cedar.

Vast numbers of Phoenician architects and builders were brought to Jerusalem to construct the temple. Hiram, a king of the Phoenician capital, Tyre, permitted 30,000 Israelites to go into the mountains and cut the cedars for the temple. It stood for more than 400 years, but in 587 B.C. the soldiers of the king of Babylon burned it. A few years later Cyrus, first of the great Persian kings, conquered Babylon and helped the Hebrews rebuild the temple, again with vast amounts of cedar.

As the centuries passed, people continued to cut and use the cedars. The Turks, who ruled Lebanon from the sixteenth century to the end of World War I, cleared vast stretches of the cedar forest, and in World War II the Allied armies cut almost all the remaining trees to build a railroad along the eastern shore of the Mediterranean.

Since then the Lebanese, even though torn by civil war, have attempted to preserve the few remaining stands of cedar, and to plant new groves of the trees. American, British, and French agencies have helped. Seeds taken from the few remaining cedars have been grown in nurseries, and the seedlings that have sprouted have been replanted in the mountains. Much of the land once covered by the cedars, however, already has been reforested by pine. Even so, a considerable area has been replanted with the young cedars.

Meanwhile, the two groves of large cedars—the most extensive of which contains about 400 trees—still stand in the northern mountains. These trees are in a very real sense witnesses to the history in which others of their species played a part, for the most ancient of the cedars in the groves are about 2,500 years old.

The Strange and the Beautiful

ONE DAY IN OCTOBER 1765, two men on horseback were riding through the wilderness along Georgia's Altamaha River, which flows to the sea between Savannah and Brunswick. They were father and son, John and William Bartram. John, then 66 years old, was famed as an explorer and naturalist, and one of the world's most respected botanists. His son, approaching 27 years of age, would follow in his footsteps, exploring and reporting the flora and fauna of the still-wild reaches of eastern North America. As they rode, the Bartrams noticed a small tree, no more than twenty feet tall, with long leaves of glossy green, beginning to redden with their autumn hue. They had never seen such a tree before, but as it was autumn, and the tree not in flower, the Bartrams, as William later wrote, "could form no opinion to what class or tribe it belonged."

Several years later, when the American colonies were rising against the British, William Bartram returned to the Altamaha country, this time in the spring. The tree he and his father had discovered was in bloom, with large white blossoms, which the younger Bartram described as "of the first order for beauty and fragrance." Impressed, he named the tree after a close associate and friend of his father's, Benjamin Franklin.

The Franklin tree, *Franklinia altamaha*, with its beautiful white flowers, was a member of the tea family. Bartram returned to observe it several times. He brought back some franklinia to the garden of rare and beautiful plants he and his father kept for study near Philadelphia, and sent others to botanists elsewhere in the United States and in Great Britain. A few other naturalists also visited the Altamaha River region to see franklinia growing in the wild, and took some for cultivation.

FRANKLINIA
flower of tree

If franklinia had not been cultivated two centuries ago, no one today would be able to see the live plant. The last time anyone reported seeing a Franklin tree growing in the wild was in 1803. Since then it has disappeared, except in cultivation.

Franklinia grew wild only along the Altamaha, at least as far as anyone knows. Perhaps ages ago it was more widespread. But, as William Bartram reported, "We never saw it grow in any other place."

No one knows why the tree disappeared. Possibly when the Bartrams discovered it, it was already a doomed plant, unable to cope with its environment as it had in the past. Perhaps elsewhere in the region more franklinia trees grew, unknown to the Bartrams, but were destroyed as woodlands were cleared. We can only guess. One thing, however, is certain. There are no more wild Franklin trees.

As far as anyone knows, the Franklin tree was the first plant in the United States to vanish from the wild. For this reason, it has become a symbol of plants in danger, and even has been commemorated on a postage stamp. It is very fitting that franklinia has become such a symbol, because it, like many of the other imperiled plants, has flowers of great

45

beauty. Sometimes, in fact, it seems as if beauty and rarity go together. Perhaps this is true, perhaps not; but there is no denying that beauty has contributed to the decrease of many types of plants, at least indirectly.

Because beauty fascinates the human mind, plants with flowers that have lovely colors or striking patterns become prizes for collectors. Some of these plants bring high prices—in the thousands of dollars. People seek them out, wherever they are found, and plunder them from the wild. The same is true of plants that for one reason or another are weird or unusual.

OCONEE BELLS

The strange and the beautiful among the plants have been collected greedily, with little thought for the future. To make matters worse, many beautiful and unusual plants have very limited habitats, in terms of either geography or environment. The small, white flowers called oconee bells, for example, grow only on a few sites in the rich mountain woodlands of four southeastern states—Georgia, the Carolinas, and Virginia. So rare it once was thought extinct, the oconee bells plant depends on the shade of the deep woods. It must have the tree shade to survive.

The southeastern mountains are a haven for many other rare wildflowers. One type of monkshood, so called because part of its purple flower is shaped like a hood, exists only in clearings scattered through the spruce and fir forests atop the southern Appalachians. The yellow flower of the Appalachian avens, which appears in midsummer, grows only on a few of the highest peaks of the Great Smokies and surrounding mountains.

MONKSHOOD

Many other wildflowers have habitats that are similarly limited. The sand myrtle and Pickering morning glory, for instance, grow only in the woodlands of the New Jersey

46

pine barrens. The barrens are a wilderness of pines, scrubby oaks, and sand which begins about 35 miles southwest of New York City and covers much of southern New Jersey. The pine woods stretch west almost to Philadelphia, and are a shrinking wilderness in the midst of a vast urban clutter.

Far to the south, in northern Florida, the woodlands of the Apalachicola National Forest resemble the pine barrens. Both regions are dotted here and there with bogs, whose waters are stained brown by the acid from peat. At the edges of bogs in a portion of the Apalachicola National Forest, grows a yellow flower on a stem almost two feet high. In all the world, those bog margins are the only home of this plant, harperocallis. California is the home of several unique and endangered plants, some of which inhabit only small regions of the state. One species of Mariposa lily, for example, exists in but a single county, San Luis Obispo, and the California rose mallow grows only at the edges of a few

SAND MYRTLE

MALLOW

GLOBE MALLOW

MARIPOSA LILY

streams and marshes. In the woodlands of Maine and nearby parts of Canada grow a few scattered patches of an extremely rare relative of the snapdragon called the Furbish lousewort. The plant gets its name because people once thought it transmitted cattle lice. This plant is so rare that when 200 of the flowers were found growing in an area to be flooded by a hydroelectric dam planned for the St. John River in Maine, the project was held up. Scientists now are trying to find out if the lousewort is as rare as believed, or perhaps more widespread.

As a rule, wildflowers are very delicate, adapted only to very specific soil, surroundings, and weather. They need just the right amount of moisture and sunlight and generally tolerate not even a slight variation in the balance. This is why wildflowers, and indeed many other wild plants, are often very difficult to transplant.

A lesson may be learned from what has happened to a small species of flowering tree, the soufrière, on the Caribbean island of St. Vincent. The species, which grows to thirty feet and produces pink flowers, once grew on a volcano, Soufrière, after which it is named. However, eruptions of the volcano at the beginning of the nineteenth century, and again early in this one, destroyed all the soufrière trees growing there. The species did not become extinct, though, because a single tree survived. It had been taken from the slopes of the volcano and transplanted to a botanical garden at a lower altitude 200 years ago. The tree is still growing there, but in all the time it has stood in the garden it has not reproduced. Scientists are not certain why, but perhaps the climate of the island's lowlands is too hot and humid for a plant that evolved on cool mountain slopes. Cuttings taken from the soufrière have been sent to England and Hawaii in hopes they will grow in these places. But if they do not, the soufrière is doomed.

The precarious nature of the balance that can mean either life or death for a plant is illustrated by how the life cycle of small tropical flowers called podostemons is linked to the cycle of high and low water in the streams they inhabit. The podostemons are related to foot-high plants called saxifrages, which grow on rocky hillsides in the United States. However, the tropical podostemons look nothing like their relatives. Instead, the podostemons resemble the mosses which encrust damp rocks in watercourses. There is a good reason for the similarity. The podostemons have adapted to living on rocks in fast-flowing streams.

During the wet seasons, when the streams are swelling, the rocks on which the podostemons live are under the water. As the dry season approaches and the water level begins to drop, the podostemons nearest the surface bud. Once the water retreats below the tops of the rocks on which the budding plants live, they flower. Eventually, high and dry, the flowers wither and release their seeds.

Because they are so dependent on the rise and fall of the water, the podostemons, many of which are rare, are threatened by anything that could change the cycle of high and low water. And that is what conservationists fear will happen if dams are built on the streams that support podostemons.

It does not take the total destruction of the environment to destroy a species of plant with a small range and very special needs. If the shady woodlands in the few places where the oconee bells grow are disturbed, for instance, the flower could vanish, even if the plants are not damaged directly. When plants have such a limited habitat, the chances are that their needs cannot be satisfied elsewhere. If the pine barrens of New Jersey are swallowed up by the urban areas around them, the chances are that the Pickering morning glory and sand myrtle which are adapted to living in the barrens will disappear.

There is no better example of how plants can become completely dependent upon a very special set of conditions than to look at species which inhabit islands, especially those far from other land. Species existing in such places have developed in isolation far removed from outside influences. Isolation tends to make species extreme, vastly different even from relatives from which they have been separated. Islands always seem to produce oddities—in the case of animals, such creatures as the giant moas of New Zealand and the dodo of Mauritius. Island plants often are odd or unique, too. On Sumatra grows a lily with a flower eight feet tall. Lobelias—plants which generally grow only a few feet high—have evolved into 35-foot-high giants in the Hawaiian Islands.

Hawaii is one of the most isolated island groups in the world, and the home of an astounding number of unique plants. Almost all of the more than 2,000 plant species native to Hawaii have no other home. As mentioned earlier, almost half are in danger—and in fact, 300 are either extinct or close to it.

The sad state of the Hawaiian plants has to do with the same condition that makes them unique—isolation. As Hawaiian species developed, they were protected by the isolation of their home from many of the enemies and competitors with which plants elsewhere had to cope. But since the coming of Europeans and Americans to Hawaii more than a century ago, the isolation of the native plants has ended.

Alien animals and plants have been introduced all over the Hawaiian Islands. Hawaiian plants have not been able to contend with the flood of invading species.

Few Hawaiian plants, for example, ever developed protective thorns and spines. So the island plants had no protection when, in the late eighteenth century, Europeans brought pigs, sheep, cattle, and goats to Hawaii. They feasted on the defenseless plants. Moreover, large numbers of goats and pigs escaped, and their descendants now run wild in many parts of the island state—while even creatures such as the wild boar have been loosed there. The foreign animals have eaten and trampled their way through the native Hawaiian vegetation.

Plants from overseas have also run wild in the Hawaiian Islands. On the island of Kauai the European blackberry has spread into the mountains, crowding out the plants that belong there. More foreign species of plants have been introduced on the Hawaiian Islands, in fact, than lived there in the first place. And all the while, people have been hacking away at the native plants, clearing land for planting crops such as sugar cane, and opening pasturage for livestock. The results have been a catastrophe, for what has happened amounts to the destruction of the plant population of a remarkable region of the earth.

Among the victims are some of the most unusual and gorgeous plants found anywhere. They include several species of the giant members of the lobelia family, which once were characteristic of Hawaiian forests. Only a handful of these trees has survived land clearance and the livestock that destroyed the young trees. A large member of the daisy family, sometimes known as the thistle tree and a native of mountain forests, is another victim of livestock. Goats which roam the Haleakala National Park on the island of Maui threaten the rare and unusual tree geranium, which grows only in a few places atop the Haleakala Volcano.

The cinder cones near the volcano once were dotted with silverswords, spectacular plants whose nine-foot-high spikes are fringed with silvery-haired leaves. The goats, together with plant collectors, have decimated this interesting species. On the beaches, development has almost exterminated a shrubby member of the bean family, *Sesbania tomentosa*, famed for its dazzling red flowers.

Like islands, mountain peaks are isolated from the regions around them. Ecologically, for that matter, mountain peaks are islands, and the plants growing on them very different from those of the surrounding lowlands. Along the tops of the Great Smoky Mountains of Tennessee and North Carolina, for example, grow spruce and fir forests unlike anything on the slopes below. To find woodlands like them, one must look far to the north, in New England and southern Canada.

Some of the peaks of the southeastern mountains have unusual concentrations of flowers. The most noted of these mountaintops is Roan Mountain, where Tennessee and North Carolina meet in the mist more than 6,000 feet above sea level. The top of Roan Mountain is a beautiful natural garden of many hundred acres. In the spring and early summer it is ablaze with the color of multitudes of wildflowers. But Roan Mountain is most famous for the vast stands of rhododendrons, which compete for the mountaintop with groves of spruce and "balds" (meadows) of oat grass. In June, when the rhododendrons bloom, the mountain is splashed with vivid reds and purples. Threatened by second-home and recreational developments, the rhododen-

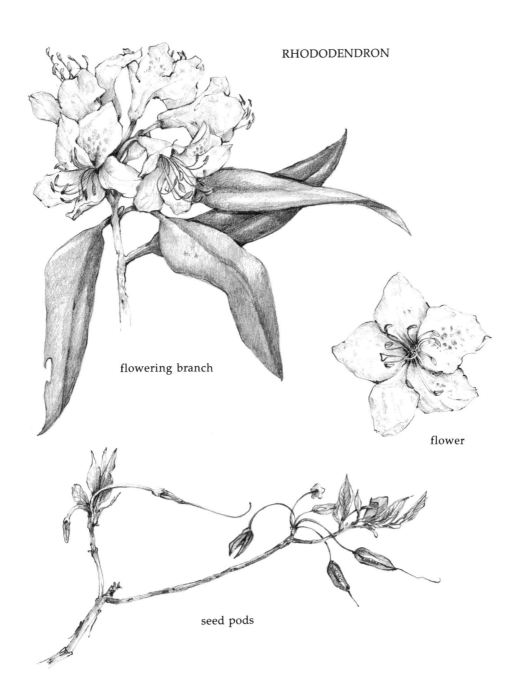

RHODODENDRON

flowering branch

flower

seed pods

dron groves of Roan Mountain are among the last of such size in the nation.

In some parts of the world, the conditions on mountains are so special that the plants growing there are as unique as those of oceanic islands. Seventy-five percent of the plants on some mountains in Venezuela, for example, grow only there. Unfortunately, many of the plants of those mountains will be destroyed before they are identified for science. All over Venezuela—throughout South America, in fact—the lush natural vegetation of the mountain forests is being cut and burned. Pressured by exploding human populations on the slopes below, farmers are being forced to clear mountainsides that are unsuitable for agriculture, but that are the only places left.

Meanwhile, plant collectors rove the Venezuelan uplands in search of rare blooms, especially the many orchids that grow there. In many ways, orchids are the most beautiful and unusual of all flowers, and what is happening to them typifies the state of such plants in the world today.

Orchids originated in the tropics about 65 million years ago, not long after the flowering plants first spread across the earth and at about the time of the last dinosaurs. From the tropics, the tiny orchid seeds—no bigger than motes of dust—were carried by the winds and on birds to almost every continent except Antarctica, and to many large oceanic islands. As the orchids were dispersed across the world they diversified into thousands of different species. All told, more than 20,000 species of orchids may have evolved naturally, and at least that many kinds have been artificially developed by plant breeders.

Throughout their vast range, orchids have adapted to an astonishing variety of habitats. They can be found above the snow line of mountains in many parts of the world. They grow at sea level, and even under the surfaces of ponds and streams. Some orchids, lacking chlorophyll, live underground. These species, usually yellow, brown, or white in color, derive their nourishment from decaying material in the soil. Other orchids, such as the increasingly rare lady's slippers of North America and Europe, grow in shady, temperate woodlands. The whorled pogonia, a green orchid, grows only in the forests of pine and oak in the Great

WHORLED POGONIA

LADY'S SLIPPER

GRASS PINK

Smoky Mountains. The grass pink finds its home in open areas of bogs and meadows of eastern North America. The prairie white-fringed orchid grows on moist open ground from the eastern seaboard to the plains states.

In the tropics, many orchids are air plants, perching on the crooks of branches or in cracks in the bark of trees, and drawing moisture from the mist and rain rather than the soil. Some tropical orchids, such as the vividly marked scorpion orchid of southeast Asia, are vines. The vanilla beans we use for flavoring come from an orchid vine that sometimes reaches a length of 200 feet.

Perhaps the most curious thing about orchids is the way many of them attract the insects which spread their pollen, and thus enable them to reproduce. Some orchids manufacture wax that bees use to build combs. When the bees visit the orchids to get the wax they are dusted with pollen, which they spread on visits to other orchids of the same species. More astonishing, however, is how some orchids have flowers that actually mimic the insects which pollinate them. The resemblance is so close that some of these orchids are named after the insects they mimic. There are "fly orchids" and "butterfly orchids," for instance, in South America.

PRAIRIE WHITE-FRINGED ORCHID

"Butterfly Orchid"

In most cases the orchid flower imitates the female insect, which lures males intent on mating. The male insects are fooled so thoroughly they actually attempt to mate with the flower, unknowingly picking up pollen as they do. Some of the orchids even emit a scent similar to that given off by the sexual glands of the female insects they resemble.

Once an orchid flower is pollinated, the portion of the stem behind the flower balloons into a capsule which can hold up to 5 million seeds, tiny dark specks that spread like powder when ripe.

Like other plant families, the orchids have members which are extremely rare in the wild. The small green orchid known as *Isotria medeoloides,* scattered in tiny colonies of a few plants each in the woodlands of the eastern United States, is so scarce only a few botanists ever have seen it. The red disa, or "pride of Table Mountain," exists in the wild only on the great flat-topped mountain which rises over Cape Town, South Africa.

Many more orchids, while not in immediate danger, are diminishing at an alarming rate because their habitat is being destroyed. The destruction of the world's tropical rain forests is a major threat to the orchid family, for most of its members inhabit the jungles of southeast Asia and the American tropics. In many parts of the United States lady's slippers of one type or another remain common, but in other portions of the country, where the woodlands have been cleared for development, these flowers are almost gone.

Lady's slippers and many tropical orchids are caught in a dangerous crunch between the destruction of their habitat and the plundering by plant hunters. Orchids—along with cacti, as will be shown in the next chapter—have suffered greatly from excessive collecting. Orchids have attracted a

Isotria medeoloides

LAELIA

vast number of dedicated hobbyists around the world. There are orchid societies in almost every country, with memberships totaling in the thousands. Many of these orchid fanciers have made great contributions to horticulture, breeding rare species and, by crossing existing ones, developing new hybrids for cultivation. The first artificial orchid hybrid was produced more than a century ago in England. But on the negative side, the fanciers' demand for orchids has encouraged collectors who have no regard for conservation of the plants they sell.

Orchid collecting has been going on around the world for centuries. Orchid hunters have combed jungles, and gone to the ends of the earth, in search of valuable new flowers, often risking their lives in the process. Entire jungles were stripped of their flowers. Early in the last century, for instance, orchids were sent to Europe from the Philippines in shipments of up to 40,000 plants each. In 1847, collectors were amazed at the quantities of an orchid known as *Laelia elegans* which they found on a small island off the coast of Brazil. Fifty years later, not one flower remained.

Today, the looting of orchids from the wild continues. The purple-stained laelia, a relative of that island orchid, lives as

PURPLE-STAINED LAELIA

an air plant in the coastal forests near Rio de Janeiro. Botanists have warned that it has been collected so extensively it may vanish from the wild. Collecting also has brought the red disa close to extinction as a wild-growing plant.

The same relentless collecting of orchids goes on in the United States. A few years ago, conservationists discovered that one dealer had uprooted 700,000 rattlesnake plantain orchids in Tennessee to sell as house plants. The rattlesnake plantain is a low-growing woodland orchid whose dark green leaves are webbed with white lines in a pattern that resembles snakeskin. American Indians once used the plant as a remedy for snakebite, and today it is a favorite for terrariums, and is thus sought after by commercial dealers. Major plant dealers often pay rural people to search the woodlands in their areas for orchids. In many places entire colonies of lady's slippers have been dug up and the plants sold to commercial collectors for a few cents each.

Some experts believe that almost all of the American orchids uprooted from their native soils and marketed by dealers die within two years. Orchids have very specific needs, particularly with regard to soil and temperature. Most of the orchids taken from the cool Venezuelan highlands, for instance, perish when brought down out of the mountains to markets in warm lowland cities. On the other hand, thousands of types of cultivated orchids, grown especially for fanciers and as houseplants, do quite well—much better "in captivity" than their wild relatives.

RATTLESNAKE PLANTAIN

Plant collectors menace another group of highly unusual plants, which also are under pressure from the destruction of their habitats. These are the carnivorous plants, which generally live in marshes, bogs, and swamps—the wetlands which are being increasingly polluted, or drained and filled. Carnivorous plants obtain a little nourishment from nitrogen in the soil, but their main food is insects. Once trapped by a carnivorous plant, an insect is digested in a manner similar to the way we digest food in our stomachs. In fact, the plants use the same digestive enzyme—a chemical called pepsinase—we do.

About fifty species of carnivorous plants inhabit the wetlands of the United States. They are grouped into three types, according to the way they trap their prey. One group is represented by the pitcher plants, which have hollow, pitcher-shaped leaves lined with hairs and filled with water. The pitcher plants lure insects with their nectar. Flies, moths, and bees, attracted by the sweet smell of the nectar, alight on the lip of the pitcher and fall into the water. The hairs within the pitcher point downward, preventing the insects from crawling up again. The water into which the insects tumble contains digestive enzymes which absorb the prey. The California pitcher plant even has a lid on it to keep prey from escaping.

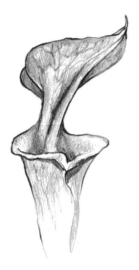

leaf funnel

PITCHER PLANT

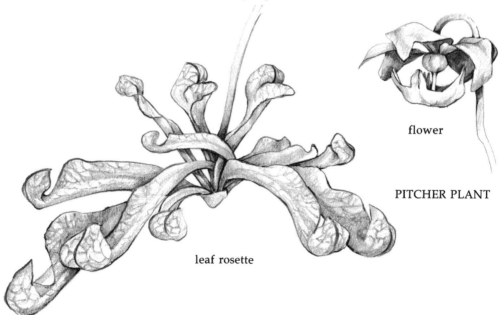

leaf rosette

flower

PITCHER PLANT

Another group of carnivorous plants catches insects by means of sticky hairs. The sundew, an inhabitant of bogs, has hairs fringing its cushiony, rounded leaves. When insects are lured to the plant by the sweet smell of the sundew, they stick to the hairs. The more they struggle, the more entangled they become, and the leaves wrap around them. Digestion is carried on by juices secreted by the hairs. The butterwort is another plant which traps insects with sticky hairs on its leaves. It is an attractive plant, with purple flowers atop long slender stems. At the base of the stems, close to the ground, the leaves of the butterwort form a rosette about two inches across. When an insect is trapped on a leaf, its edges curl up and over the prey, but very slowly. It takes almost a week for the leaf to enclose the insect and digest it. The butterwort takes only very tiny insects, even smaller than ants.

The most famous of carnivorous plants is one that catches insects with a trap that resembles a yawning mouth. It is the Venus's flytrap, which has two-lobed leaves hinged in the middle and edged with stiff "teeth." When the trap formed by a leaf is open, it looks for all the world like the maw of a predatory animal, an impression furthered by the reddish color of the lining of the "mouth." Insects are drawn to the trap by the color and a scented secretion of the leaf. On the lining of the trap are tiny hairs which, when touched by an insect, trigger the trap. The two lobes snap shut, the teeth on their edges interlock, and the insect is trapped, unless it is small enough to wriggle between the teeth. Over a period of almost two weeks, the prey is digested. Then the trap opens again, and the remains of the insect are dropped to the earth.

Venus's flytraps, pitcher plants, and butterworts are highly marketable plants, for not only are they curiosities, but

leaf

SUNDEW

leaf detail
enlargement

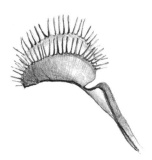

VENUS'S FLYTRAP
leaf detail

61

they are quite colorful. Several types of pitcher plants are decreasing to the danger point, and so are some varieties of butterwort. But it is the Venus's flytrap that really is in trouble.

Business in flytraps is brisk. Countless numbers of the plants have been sold as novelties, even by mail order. Some of these flytraps have been cultivated, but most are taken from the wild. That alone might not be so bad if the Venus's flytrap were widespread. But it has an extremely small range—only the sandy coastal plain of the Carolinas, and there the flytrap is confined to only a handful of bogs with acid soil. Even if the flytrap were left alone it would be considered a plant vulnerable to extinction. With each raid of collectors upon the flytrap colonies, the chances of its survival in the wild dim.

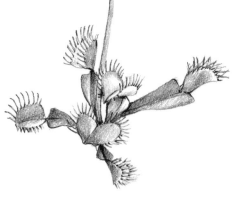

VENUS'S FLYTRAP

The Disappearing Desert Dwellers

A FOREST in the desert? It exists. In fact, there are many desert forests, especially in the southwestern United States and adjacent regions of Mexico. Large expanses of desert there are dotted with saguaros and other big cacti. They have enough size to qualify as trees, and grow thickly enough for their stands to be considered forests.

The cactus forests are unusual, and in many cases unique, because cacti are often prisoners of very special habitats. In the beginning of this book, it was noted that the giant saguaro grows only in the Sonora Desert. And within that desert the saguaro's needs are very precise. The giant cactus prospers only in rocky or gravelly soils, and generally at altitudes between 2,000 and slightly more than 3,500 feet. In the northern part of its range, moreover, the cactus is found on slopes with a southern exposure, where it is warmed by the sun and shielded from the worst winter cold. At the other end of its range, where the climate is quite hot year round, the saguaro grows on the cooler northern slopes. And in between, the direction the slope faces makes no difference. In portions of its range which have the least rainfall—only a few inches yearly—saguaros follow the washes, stream beds which are dry most of the time but fill with water during rare rainstorms.

63

Many other cacti are restricted to even smaller habitats than the huge saguaro. At the other end of the cactus size spectrum is a small plant, known as *Pediocactus peeblesianus peeblesianus*, which is no bigger than a thimble, and which has a similarly tiny range. It exists only within an area of a few miles in Navajo County, Arizona, and even within that tract is so scarce it is almost impossible to find.

About 1,000 species of cacti inhabit the Americas, and they are not all desert plants. Cacti can be found on the beaches of New England and in the wilderness of central Canada as well as in the sands of the southwestern states and Mexico. It is in the desert, however, that cacti grow in greatest variety and profusion.

Like other desert plants, the cacti have adapted to the extreme conditions of life in a harsh environment in which, in order to survive, a plant must cope with a lack of water. One way cacti do this is by spreading roots out over a large area, close to the surface, so they can absorb as much moisture as possible. Some cactus roots extend for a circumference of fifty feet around the base of the plant. This means that the plant can draw moisture—from dew, for instance—from a very large area. Other cacti push their roots deep into the ground, sometimes thirty feet or more, to tap subterranean water supplies. When water is available, cacti store up huge amounts of the precious fluid. The trunk of the saguaro is pleated, and can expand like an accordion to accommodate a reservoir of water. When it rains, a saguaro trunk may swell a foot or more as it soaks up moisture, like a giant sponge. A six-ton saguaro can absorb a ton of water.

But for all their ability to get along under such difficult conditions, the cacti may be the most endangered of all large families of plants. More than a quarter of the species native to the United States could be extinct within a few years if they are not scrupulously protected. Most imperiled cacti are threatened by the same sorts of pressures, all of which arise from human activities. What is happening to the largest of them all, the saguaro, provides a grim example of the dangers facing these marvelous and interesting plants.

First of all, the saguaro is threatened because the desert it inhabits is being changed on a broad scale, upsetting its environmental balance. Livestock have overgrazed vast stretches of desert land on which vegetation, once destroyed, finds it almost impossible to grow again. Cattle have destroyed countless young saguaros, which are only a few inches tall for several years. Increasingly, the desert landscape has been covered with housing developments and tourist resorts, particularly in recent years, as the desert states have become a popular region for retirement and vacations. Housing units have spread out into the desert from such cities as Tucson, Arizona, like ink on a blotter. Off-the-road recreational vehicles are another threat to the desert, as they plow over the sand and gravel, crushing small plants, and bowling over larger ones.

Even if such activities did not directly damage the saguaros—and they do—the disruption of the environment still would threaten the existence of the towering cactus. No species lives alone; all are part of the web of life, and when one strand of the web is damaged, the ill effects may spread. By wiping out coyotes, rattlesnakes, and other predators, people have contributed to a rise in the populations of small rodents, which the coyotes and snakes helped control. Some of the rodents feed on the young saguaros and the seeds. The saguaro also is in a situation similar to that of the oconee bells discussed in the last chapter: Shade is important to the

65

big cactus, not all the time but at the very beginnings of its life. The saguaro seed will not sprout unless it is shaded. If the scrubby paloverde, mesquite, and similar desert plants which provide the vital shade are eliminated from an area, saguaros cannot reproduce there. The saguaro, in turn, is important to many other living things that share its desert community.

It is impossible to tell how many saguaros have been eliminated by human abuse of the desert, but the number must be immense. The construction of a pond for refuse of a mining operation near Tucson not long ago flooded hundreds of acres of saguaros, and that type of destruction occurs in much of the giant cactus's range. Countless other saguaros have been damaged and destroyed even more senselessly. Many people seem unable to pass by a big saguaro without chopping off an arm, carving a hole in it, or peppering it with gunshots. One man was even caught shooting down saguaros with a machine gun.

At the same time, other people like saguaros too much for the good of the cactus. The saguaro is a prime target of plant collectors, not just commercial collectors but people who want a cactus or two for their homes or gardens. Increasingly, saguaros have been a big business for commercial dealers. A saguaro with two or three arms brings a price of several hundred dollars. Even people who live in saguaro country will pay dealers ten dollars a foot for the big cacti, and overseas, where the demand is booming, the price is four times that figure. Hundreds of saguaros are being shipped regularly to Europe, and also to Japan, where buyers pay the highest prices.

Cactus collecting, in fact, has grown to truly alarming proportions, and not just with regard to the saguaro. Entire populations of cactus are picked clean by collectors, who scour the deserts in search of particularly rare species. The collectors are persistent and spend long days in the sizzling sun in search of their prizes. A few years ago, for example, a woman turned up at a national convention of cactus fanciers with several of the Navajo County *Pediocactus* plants sewed to the brim of her hat—yet even experienced botanists have a hard time finding the button-size cactus amidst the sand and rocks of its home.

The situation has become so serious that agencies charged with the conservation of natural resources are beginning to take action to control the plundering of cacti in the desert states. Of all the states, Arizona has taken the lead. In 1972 Arizona put into effect a tough "native plant law," which protects scores of plants from uncontrolled collecting. Penalties for violating the law include heavy fines and even jail— and the state has several "cactus cops," gun-toting officers bound to enforce the protection of plants.

The cactus cops cover more than 113,000 square miles of territory and have apprehended dozens of illegal collectors annually. "Cactus rustling," which often takes place by the light of the moon, has become a thriving illegal business, worth $1 million a year.

The rustlers are clever, and state agents must use their wits to catch them with their contraband cacti. One rustler caught by the agents had 357 cacti, a third of them saguaros, under the false floor of a truck covered with wood. Another had illegal cacti underneath a load of cacti for which, under law, he had been issued collecting permits. Regular police units also help combat the cactus rustlers. In April 1976, state highway patrol officers caught a man who had more than 300 barrel cacti in his vehicle.

If the heedless destruction and collecting continue, many cacti will be preserved only on government sanctuaries. Indeed, some well-known cacti live almost entirely on such preserves. One of the most important is the Organ Pipe Cactus National Monument, located in southwestern Arizona, on the Mexican border. It is a rugged, spectacular region of stark hills sculpted out of volcanic rock, where summer temperatures often top 100° F. The monument gets its name from a cactus which is a relative of the saguaro, and whose clusters of stems, sometimes twenty feet high, resemble banks of organ pipes.

Like the saguaro, the organ-pipe is long-lived, and sometimes stands for a century and a half. It needs an extremely warm climate, and hardly exists in the United States outside of the monument, which is protected from the most severe winter weather by mountains to the north. Even in the monument, the organ-pipes grow only on slopes facing south. The saguaros in the monument—which outnumber the organ-pipes—are able to exist on slopes of any exposure.

The Organ Pipe Cactus National Monument also provides a haven for what probably is the rarest large cactus in the United States, the senita. Related to the organ-pipe, it is about the same size and general appearance. It is found scattered throughout the Sonora Desert in Mexico, all the way into Baja California, but only about fifty senita cacti, virtually all of them in the monument, exist north of the United States border.

It might seem as if the cacti of the Organ Pipe Cactus National Monument are forever safe, but that may not be completely true. Several large and powerful companies still claim mining rights to parts of the monument, and ranchers still loose cattle and horses to graze there. Conservationists want to stop any attempt to mine the area and remove the livestock, so that the cacti and other plants the monument was established to protect will truly be safeguarded for the future.

What if some species of cactus vanish? Will it make any real difference to nature as a whole, or to human welfare? That is a difficult question to answer with precision. It often is impossible to determine all of the consequences of the extinction of a species until after it happens. Many of the interrelationships that make up the web of life are so complex or unclear that they still escape our understanding. However, you may be able to satisfy yourself about the question by imagining, for a moment, that you are spending a day and a night in another national monument dedicated to a cactus, in this case the saguaro.

The Saguaro National Monument, established in 1933, consists of two sections, a 98-square-mile part known as Rincon Mountain, east of the city of Tucson, and the 22-square-mile Tucson Mountain section, to the west of the city. Both sections are small samples of what the immense reaches of the Sonora Desert are like in a natural state. The altitude of the monument ranges from about 3,000 feet to more than 8,000 feet, and within that range the communities of plants are divided into zones. The mountaintops are forested with Douglas fir, white fir, and ponderosa pine. As the altitude decreases, pines mix with scrub oak and juniper. Lower yet, tough desert grasses appear, and finally, below about 4,000 feet, begins a zone called the desert-scrub belt. This zone is desert in a true sense, and is the home of the giant saguaros.

From a distance, the tall saguaros can be seen rising like great, green columns from the gravelly, rocky slopes, climb-

SAGUARO CACTUS

ing the hillsides and filling the ravines with their straight forms. In among the old giants are the younger saguaros, of varying ages, and sizes. And scattered about are the remains of other saguaros, long dead. Their pulpy, spongy tissues have decayed and vanished, but the woody ribs that served as the frameworks for their mighty columns remain. Gray and dry, they rustle like ancient skeletons when a hot breeze brushes the desert. The ribs are useful for building shelters, as the Indians of the area have long known.

The giant cacti grow amidst a welter of smaller cacti and tough, leathery-leaved trees and shrubs. The ground is studded with stout, spine-covered barrel cacti, and covered with clumps of prickly pear and hedgehog cacti. Paloverde trees, mesquite, and creosote bushes form broken patches of scrub around the cacti, which tower above all else.

During the heat of the day, the kingdom of the saguaro is quiet. Perhaps, down among the rocky walls of a canyon, a collared lizard scuttles into a cleft, or a gila monster hauls its thickset, pink-and-black form into the shade of an overhang. On spring days there is more activity by animals of the saguaro forest, especially birds, many of which use the saguaro as an apartment house when it is time to nest.

Red-tailed hawks build their bulky nests of sticks among the arms of the giant cactus. Abandoned hawk nests, cradled in the arms of the huge plant, sometimes serve another powerful winged hunter, the great horned owl, when it is time for it to have and rear young. When it is time to nest, the gilded flicker and the gila woodpecker drill holes in the saguaros, pecking away at the fleshy tissue, making deep pockets in the cactus for nest chambers. The cactus responds by secreting sap around the lining of the hole, sealing off the exposed pulp so it will not release any precious moisture.

The holes made by the flickers and woodpeckers often have double use. After the hole drillers depart, other birds use them. Sparrow hawks, purple martins, and flycatchers all are willing to take over abandoned cavities in the saguaro. And so is one of the most attractive little birds of all found on the desert: the elf owl, whose range parallels that of the saguaro. No larger than a sparrow, this round-headed, big-eyed night hunter not only nests in the old woodpecker holes, but even when not rearing a family roosts in them by day. By night the elf owl ventures forth to find its prey, which consists almost entirely of insects.

Sunset in saguaro country is a sight never to be forgotten. The sky reddens, like coals on a hearth, and is splashed with purple. Shadows march over the slopes and flood the canyons. Rank by rank the saguaros darken, their columnar forms seeming even more awesome. Finally the shadows reach the ridge lines, where the saguaros are few because they are easily toppled by the wind. The lone saguaros that crown the ridges are the last to darken, but soon they too lose their green color and stand as solitary, shadowed sentinels against the fiery sky.

When the night falls, things begin to happen. The kangaroo rats emerge from their hiding places to prance upon the sand. The rattlesnakes and kit foxes hunt the rats. Mule deer materialize as if from nowhere. Peccary herds root on the desert floor. Bobcats and pumas prowl.

In May and early June, a magnificent event occurs. At the ends of the arms of the mature saguaros, large cup-shaped flowers blossom into creamy fullness. Each flower blooms for only 24 hours, in the brilliance of the sun and the darkness of the desert night. During the day, the white-winged dove is drawn to the nectar of the flowers. As the

flower bud

opening flower

SAGUARO CACTUS

flower

dove lands and dips its head into the blooms, the saguaro's pollen dusts the bird's feathers. The bird will transfer the pollen to other flowers, and insure fertilization of the cacti.

By night, other pollinators take over—insects that fly by dark, and most important of all, the long-nosed bat. This nectar feeder picks up pollen as it visits the flowers that bloom white in the blackness, and as it flits from flower to flower it makes possible the rise of new generations of saguaro.

The saguaro flowers fruit, and ripen by midsummer. The fruits of the saguaro, like those of many other cacti, have green skins, touched with a blush of red, and red pulp, heavily loaded with seeds. Many birds, including the white-winged dove, feed on the pulp of the fruit. When the fruit falls to the desert floor, it becomes a feast for the mammal tribe. The mule deer dine on the sweet, red pulp. The peccaries gobble up whatever fruit they find. In some places the rare desert bighorn sheep come down from the crags to feed on what the saguaro has let fall to the earth. And the desert rodents eat until they are near bursting. Even the coyotes sample the fruit.

When the saguaro fruit are ripe and still on the plant, the Papago Indians who live near the monument use long poles to harvest the gift of the huge plant. While some of the people pick the fruit, others boil what has already been harvested in steaming pots set over outdoor fires, making syrup. The fruit is also dried, made into cakes, and eaten fresh. The Papago people are not the only ones to know how sweet and juicy are the fruits of cacti. Italians and other Mediterranean peoples relish the prickly pear fruit, which resembles that of the saguaro. Prickly pear fruit can be found for sale in food markets in almost every American city

SAGUARO CACTUS

fruit forming
beneath dead flower

with a large number of Italian-Americans.

The saguaro is an important part of its environment, touching the lives of all sorts of other living things, from insects to people. But so is every other species of plant, even those so small they are but specks hidden in the soil or beneath the surface of the sea. Can we afford the disappearance of any species? Decide for yourself.

Saving the Plants

ABOUT 160 MILES southeast of Nairobi, Kenya, near the town of Mutomo, a steep, rocky ridge rises more than 1600 feet above the flat, dry landscape. Much of the area around the ridge is dusty and barren. The vegetation has been eaten by goats and sheep, and the soil eroded—both by wind, during long periods of drought, and by violent rainstorms that signal the end of the dry spells. The rocky walls and boulders on the ridge, however, are crowned with vegetation. More than a hundred species of trees, shrubs, and other plants once common throughout the entire area cover a tract of about 120 acres on the ridge, making it an island of survival.

The value of the ridge was recognized by conservationists and local officials in the mid-1960s. With the help of an international conservation organization, the World Wildlife Fund, the ridge was set aside as a preserve—the first sanctuary in Africa established specifically to protect plants.

Establishment of the Mutomo Plant Sanctuary was a sign of increasing awareness on the part of conservationists and governments, from a local to an international level, that they must act decisively to save rare plants, just as they have to save endangered animals. Rare plants need the same types of programs to insure their survival as animals in danger—

75

ranging from creation of sanctuaries to breeding in "captivity." Over the years, of course, there have been campaigns to save various species, such as the redwoods and the cedars of Lebanon, but the organized, international effort to save the plants is just beginning.

First, there is a need to identify the species of plants that are in danger, and to find out what threatens them. This is an awesome task, considering the immense number of species involved, and especially since many are still unknown to science. The effort is well under way, in this country and elsewhere in the world.

In 1973, Congress passed a new Endangered Species Act, which covered imperiled plants as well as animals. The new law ordered the Smithsonian Institution, our national museum, to develop a list of plants that needed protection. After examination by the Interior Department, and after public hearings, the plants that are deemed in danger will receive the same legal protection as endangered and threatened species of animals.

Meanwhile, most of the states have begun the long process of surveying the plants that grow within their borders to see how the various species are faring. Measures are being enacted to protect plants which are rare in certain localities, even if the species to which they belong are not endangered on a broad scale. In New York State, for instance, the twinflower is protected in the Catskill Mountain region, where it is scarce, but not in the Adirondack Mountains to the north, where the pink wildflower is not imperiled.

The same types of efforts are under way in Europe. Late in 1976, European scientists completed the first list of plants needing protection on that continent. The survey covered only plants that are threatened throughout their ranges, not species in danger locally. Even so, the botanists from all over Europe who contributed to the study came up with more than 1300 species.

On a worldwide basis, the enormous job of listing all the plant species vulnerable to extinction will take years. It is being coordinated by the International Union for the Conservation of Nature and Natural Resources (I.U.C.N.), which has carried on the same process for rare wild animals. Botanists from virtually every country in the world are taking part in the program, which is coordinated at the Royal Botanical Gardens in Great Britain. Special panels of scientists who are experts on particular groups of plants have been assigned to examine the problems which face these groups. The arrangement is based on what the I.U.C.N. has done with endangered groups of animals. Just as the organization has special panels for the wild cats and the crocodilians, it has groups of experts concentrating on specific kinds of plants such as orchids and palms.

Meanwhile, as the establishment of the Mutomo Plant Sanctuary demonstrates, the importance of plant preserves has gained wide recognition. More preserves like the Saguaro National Monument and Sequoia National Park are needed—not only in the United States, but elsewhere as well.

A major step in this direction was taken in 1976 when the president of Costa Rica established as a preserve almost 200 square miles of rain forest on his country's Osa Peninsula, which juts into the Pacific Ocean. The vast and undisturbed forest stretches over lowlands and up into the mountains, is dotted in places by fresh-water lagoons, and is rimmed by a combination of sandy beaches, marshes, and rocky shores. The forest, largest protected region of its kind in Central

America, contains many large trees more than 150 feet tall and, scientists believe, many rare plants.

The Costa Rican preserve is particularly important because it contains more than twenty different types of natural communities, in their entirety. One problem with the creation of many of the large preserves has been that they often contain only portions of ecological units, such as individual wetlands or forests. This decreases the value of such preserves, because by breaking up natural units they disrupt the web of life so important to the survival of the species they are supposed to protect. By preserving entire ecological units, the Costa Rican Sanctuary should insure that even the rarest plants within its boundaries will reproduce. At the same time, it also is large enough to protect many rare wild animals which need considerable room to live. In the green corridors of the forest roam jaguars and pumas. Tapirs and giant anteaters forage in the brush. American crocodiles and caimans haunt the rivers, and overhead circle the harpy eagles, largest of all the world's eagles.

Some plants, however, are so endangered that they cannot be saved by only the preservation of habitat. The round-leafed birch probably is one of these. And all the sanctuaries in the world, for instance, would not have saved franklinia if it had not been cultivated. Realizing this, the I.U.C.N. and other conservation organizations concerned with plants are establishing a network of botanical gardens, universities, and research institutions at which rare plants can be propagated so that their species will survive if they disappear from the wild.

Ironically, plant collectors could contribute to this campaign. Sometimes, for example, it is impossible to save colonies of rare plants from construction, dam building, and similar hazards. In such cases, the only way to preserve the colonies is to remove them and take the chance that at least a few of the plants will live. The plants that do survive can be placed in botanical gardens or similar institutions, for breeding or possible transplantation to other wild sites suited to them.

Another way collectors could help is by gathering the seeds of wild plants instead of taking the plants themselves from their habitat. Most plants produce many more seeds than eventually sprout. By taking some of the seeds from rare plants and growing them, plant dealers and fanciers could have plenty of specimens for their own use, while insuring that the wild populations survived.

For Further Reading

Endangered Rare and Uncommon Wildflowers Found in the Southern National Forests. Pamphlet, U.S. Department of Agriculture, U.S. Forest Service, 1720 Peachtree Road NW, Atlanta, Georgia 30309.

Fisher, James, et al. *Wildlife in Danger.* New York: Viking Press, Inc. 1969.

Hausman, Ethel Hinckley. *Beginner's Guide to Wild Flowers.* New York: G. P. Putnam's Sons, 1948.

Richards, Paul W. *The Life of the Jungle.* New York: McGraw-Hill Book Company, Inc., 1970.

Index

Numbers in *italics* refer to illustrations.

Designed by Kohar Alexanian
Set in 11 pt. Palatino
Composed by TriStar Graphics
Printed by The Murray Printing Company
HARPER & ROW, PUBLISHERS, INCORPORATED